302

Published by Spines
ISBN: 979-8-89383-789-6

# 302

SENECA WILLOUGHBY

*Helping his mother cope with her mental disorder. He is befriended by a nurse that accused him of rape. He must have another sexual encounter with his accuser, to prove his innocence.*

# CONTENTS

# ACKNOWLEDGMENTS

First, I would like to thank GOD, for this opportunity. I also would like to thank my family and friends, for standing by me through all my ups, and downs.

Thank you

Seneca Willoughby

# CHAPTER
# ONE

Troublesome. A doctor's appointment today for Ms. Mobily after receiving the sad news, which would cause my life to never be the same. March 23, 2020, was a gloomy morning in North Philadelphia filled with clouds and rain. As I leapt over the puddles of water pouring down the street, I hurried to the passenger door, reaching for the handle to help assist Mom out of the car and into the clinic. As her caregiver, due to age and mobility, one of my tasks was getting her to the doctor's appointment on time.

Escorting her into the doctor's office after hearing her name called over the intercom, I turned to leave the office once she was seated and comfortable to begin her assessment with the psychologist. The doctor asked me kindly, "Are you available to stay and sit in on the session?"

"Sure," I answered, and I went to sit down in the chair next to my mom, reaching out to hold her hand.

It would be the first time sitting in a session with her, not knowing what I would be exposed to or if Mom wanted to share her mental challenges with me, but it was nothing I could not handle when it came to Mom. Dr. G. started discussing symptoms of mental illness disorder and the severity of it. Mom was suffering from Schizophrenia and Paranoia. I asked Dr. G. to keep me updated on her status.

"Hi Ms. Mobily, how are you today?"

She answered, "A little wet from the rain but I am fine."

"Yeah, it's raining cats and dogs out there."

"Shall we begin?" Dr. G. asked Mom.

"Yes, I'm ready to start."

The doctor began to ask questions about the presence of two people that bully Mom daily, people that she can only see.

"Yes," Mother responded, "they are standing in front of me looking down at Seneca."

This was a surprise to me because I didn't see anything, but at home, I would hear her speaking aggressively, arguing with herself. Which is normal for me because she did it since I was 5 years old. However, I would hear Mom shout out names such as her sisters, my brother, and me or people that were dead she once knew.

She had a mental breakdown some years ago when I was a child. Mom was about 25 years of age; I was too young to understand. I just know one day she quit her job as a beautician at Toss It Up, the family business owned by my aunt Jazz because of a disagreement. Mom turned to drugs and started using crack cocaine along with other illicit drugs. Eventually, she got clean, stopped using, and started to attend church.

So, I thought she was battling her demons when shouting and acting out. Hearing of these people I never knew of, that existed inside of her mind was unimaginable.

"Doctor, yes, at times your mother tells me they don't allow her to leave her room. In the mornings, she holds her bladder until they allow her out to use the bathroom, causing her to go on herself at times."

"Wow," I responded with concern. "What option in treatment would be best for Mom?"

In conclusion, the doctor suggested having her 302. I'm told that to have her get treatment, she must be proven a danger to herself or others in a physical manner. Mother was always confrontational. Whenever a tenant moved into the property with her, she would chase them off because her mental illness became out of control. Eating their food and telling them, "This is my house, get out," and "I am king." I would replace items to avoid conflict, but they would rather move out.

This meant that I would have to say I was the victim of a violent act at the hands of her. She wasn't, but I would have to call the police and say that she tried to harm me by pointing a knife in my direction and threatening to cut my throat while making dinner. I struggled with this decision for a week; however, I was doing more harm than good by prolonging matters. As the week continued, I noticed the symptoms of aggression getting stronger with her behavior.

Keeping a blue stick by her bed to fight these evil spirits attacking her in her sleep. I'd asked her because I noticed blue marks on the wall left from her trying to hit them. The police came, handcuffed her, and placed her in a paddy wagon. The officers instructed me that she would be taken to the hospital, and I could follow them or call for visiting hours. As they pulled off, I couldn't help feeling like a rat. I mean, the lowest form of life imaginable on earth. But on the other hand, it's not about me. After twenty years of this mental illness not being treated, the mother will get the help and treatment that only a medical facility can provide for her.

I remember Mom telling me stories of her tough upbringing as a child. Born in Philadelphia in the late 1950s and raised in a single-parent household by her mother Francis, along with two big sisters and an older brother, in a two-story home. Often left alone at home to fend for herself was overwhelming for a six-year-old little girl. Cooking, washing clothes, and doing her hair for school was challenging, with Francis at work full-time as a bartender to make ends meet.

The children were left unsupervised without food, often to govern themselves. Her older two sisters and brother, teenagers busy out in the streets looking for opportunities for themselves. The abandonment was freedom but left Mom lonely and afraid. Making up invisible friends and talking to them when alone in the house was how she filled the void.

One afternoon, Mom recalled as a child, it was raining and thundering really bad outside, and she felt the house shake. Afraid, she went outside on the porch until someone returned home. Hungry, anxiously waiting and crying in fear not knowing the whereabouts of her siblings or the time her mother would return home. She looked up to the sky, and the sun appeared, shining down through the clouds. The rain stopped but only in front of the porch where she sat.

Beginning to calm down, staring in amazement at what she had seen as if God was looking after her. Encouraged, she went back in the house and made a syrup sandwich to feed her hunger. She later went to her room, got in bed, pulling the covers over her eyes as the raindrops tapped the window. As Mom got older, she became spiritual, in the name of Christ Jesus.

Tyrone, her older brother, became a stone-cold killer at the young age of fourteen in the streets of Philly. Hired to perform hits on rival gang leaders and extort money from business owners, he was killed before turning twenty-one. Drugged by friends, then shot up over 26 times, he was found DOA in an apartment. I wish I had a chance to meet him. Mom would tell me stories about him, like how he would come home late after being in the streets for days to pick me up out of the crib and kiss me because he fathered several girls. He made Mom promise to name me after him, considering that, she did my middle name. I wish I could remember him. Love you, Unc.

# TWO

Mother's blackout time was up after seven days, which meant she could now have visitors and receive clothing along with personal items. I used the time to myself wisely, getting rest and rehabbing the property. Mom expected the stay to be thirty days pending a review. It's been a week since I've seen her, so I don't know what to expect during the visit regarding her physical or mental condition. When I think of psychiatric wards, I can only reflect on movies that depict strapped beds, padded rooms, and overly medicated patients roaming the halls.

As I exited the elevator, the smell of sickness overwhelmed my nose. It smelled like death, and the temperature felt as if you were baking in an oven. Maybe it was the top floor, and the windows were locked and barred to prevent escapes. I followed the wax linoleum floor design, tucking half of my face into my shirt collar to try to breathe. I lifted my head just enough to observe the posted signs and rooms of patients.

Some rooms were decorated with pictures and personal items such as robes and slippers; however, the rooms reeked of foul body odor. I headed to the receptionist to inform them that I was there to visit my mother, Ms. Mobley. She instructed me on which wing and the location where I would find her. As I made my way down the hall, patients were roaming in their medical gowns and socks. They were friendly and kind, though their mental instability was evident through their repetitive speech, loud uncontrolled laughter, and erratic body movements. It wasn't threatening or intimidating, but they smelled awful, causing my face to frown.

I sat in the visiting area where a TV was mounted on the wall. Tables and chairs were spread out into small groups due to coronavirus precautions. As they brought her in, I stood up to greet her.

"Hi, Mom." We hugged and smiled. She appeared calm and relaxed, aware of her surroundings, and then asked when she was leaving. This was the first time I'd seen her this way in my forty years of life. We sat and began to speak about how she felt and how the staff was treating the patients. Mom introduced me to one of the nurses, named Naomi, who she liked.

"Hi, Ms. Mobley, who is this?"

'My youngest son, Seneca."

"Hello, I'm Naomi, nice to meet you."

"Hello, nice to meet you as well."

"I love Ms. Mobley; she is definitely a joy to have here."

"Thanks," I explained. "Mom is all I have, even though our relationship has been estranged."

A couple of years back, I had made a business decision to include her in my LLC property investments. My intention was to use the money from refinancing inherited real estate property she was awarded after taking her sister to court. To improve her quality of life, I wanted to incorporate her into my real estate investments of buying and flipping houses. Her investment would yield a monthly payment along with a portion of the sale on rehab properties, providing income and wealth for the rest of her life.

Instead, Mom went around telling anyone who would listen that I stole from her. I paid no attention to the rumor because I knew the truth; however, having your mom say this about you does cause embarrassment. The tenants renting from her that I placed in the property, friends of mine, and family, all because I asked for my initial investment back of $10,000 after renovating and paying all associated costs to facilitate a home refinance valued at $70,000. The property rent is valued at $2,500 a month with all the bills current. The final payout after the debt was paid on her credit report was $58,000. It was the most money she ever had at one time in her life, with A1 credit, along with a monthly income of $1,500 after bills were paid.

When expecting to receive repayment, I was greeted by my brother telling me I was charging mom too much. I felt I didn't have to explain myself to anyone about my money, especially to someone who knew what was going on and did nothing to help physically or financially to cut costs. But since you are my brother, I'm going to give you the benefit of the doubt. I showed itemized receipts for materials, labor, property insurance, and two months of deposit money.

Some costs I never included were my personal labor, gas, mileage, and opportunity cost. This did nothing to resolve the issue, and we began to argue and exchange threatening words. Mom always played us against one another. In my eyes, he was jealous that I could handle her whole situation without needing his help. Zek then admitted to stealing from me over the years, as I trusted him to bag up the coke and separate the re-up money. Hoping to get a reaction out of me, he laughed it off, hearing him prove what I already knew.

However, I visited my mother often, bringing her favorite food and enough to feed the entire floor. Everyone was excited and happy because their family didn't visit. Mom was proud that I thought of others while thinking of her; I just wanted everyone to know that she was loved and cared for by her family. Even though I was all the family she had at the time, I thought my brother was serving a 5-year sentence with three years in. Her sisters no longer spoke or cared because of the collateral damage she caused to their lives, something I later experienced at her hands.

My aunts got into a terrible family dispute over a property their younger sister was renting. Aunt Jazmin wanted to increase the rent, and Alexis could not afford it. This became an issue because Alexis's husband, a prison guard, got arrested for bringing drugs into the prison. This caused financial distress, meaning she and my two cousins had to get out. Even though the property was Section 8, and "Jaz" rent was $35 a month, Jaz had sublet it to "Lex" for a higher amount, profiting off it illegally.

My grandmother called my mom about the matter and asked her to help put a stop to it by talking to her older sister Jaz. It turned out for the worst, with them at each other's throats. Mom ended up exposing Jaz to the newspaper, and she was charged and fined heavily by the courts. The fighting between them caused a rift in the family for over 35 years, and it's been this way ever since.

When Mom targeted me, it was as if she had it out for me since birth. Her attitude was viewed with disdain toward my presence. I have seen the demon that possesses my mother's body. One early evening, while standing on the corner of the old neighborhood with the fellas, a car stopped at the corner sign. Viewing the driver, Zek, Sr., front passenger Mother, and rear passenger Zek, I waved and spoke as the others accompanied me as they headed in the direction of our old home.

I noticed they parked in front, and Mom got out of the car. I began to walk up the street toward the abandoned property we once occupied as a family. Not wanting the neighbors and friends to notice the tension between us, I faked it and played it off as if we were on good terms. However, I knew she was running a smear campaign, which could have been detrimental to my reputation. Mom gave the money to me, but it was accompanied by lies, slander, and deception of my character.

She put the key in the front door, unaware of my presence standing at the bottom of the steps. When I spoke, I noticed a lizard-like demon entity turn toward me as her head delayed and followed. Our eyes locked as I stood there, motionless. Mom started cussing and swearing at me, "What the fuck do you want? I gave you the money!" Shocked, I gathered myself as I realized they were here to execute my plan to rehab the property with the funds left from the refinance. Feeling defeated and lost, I had never seen them together as a family unit.

Now that I sacrificed my time, energy, and financial resources, they stand united against me. As I was leaving from the visit, I was approached by a staff member as she inserted her key into the elevator control. She said, "My colleague is interested in meeting you; she thinks you're cute. I think you are fine too, but I'm married. Here, take this paper; it has her number on it, and she's too shy to write her name." As she reached toward me, she repeated, "You're going to call? You're going to call? You better call; if not, next time you visit, I'm not going to use my key to call the elevator for you." She was laughing and blushing. I thought, not now, attention is cool, but I'm in a midlife crisis.

# THREE

99 problems and a chick and one, I'm overwhelmed with my personal life. Sleeping with the enemy after twenty-three years. Kala's relationship had not always been in a state of turmoil. But her aiming a .44 magnum at me at 10 am one morning, trying to kill me, was crazy. I wasn't certain why she was in an upset mood—could it have been my late return home? She slapped me as I got out of the shower, after she wiped off, flushed the toilet, and washed her hands.

In shock, my reflex caused me to slap her back. Storming out, she returned in a rage, kicking in the bathroom double door and screaming, "Pussy, I'm going to kill you!" I quickly closed and locked the doors, hiding alongside the Italian marble sink. I wasn't sure if Kala knew how to use a .44 Magnum revolver. As I looked toward the second-story window, preparing to jump out of it to escape with my life, adrenaline raced through me, expecting to hear a loud bang.

Intrigued by the utter silence, I opened the doors to find Jr. standing next to his mother, armed and in danger. I bear-hugged her to the floor and snatched the gun out of her gripped right hand as she yelled, "Let me go!" I wondered if our son's overnight guest could hear us tussle. "Can you imagine the outcome of this situation?" I said through tight lips, pinning her down with my 250 pounds of body weight. "There are kids in here and you want to kill me?" I looked up to tell Jr. to leave the room and get back to his friends. As I stood up to get off Kala, I then left the bedroom, closing the doors to hide the pistol in a spot she wouldn't find. Leaving it under my side of the bed between the mattress was no longer a good idea. I had the gun for protection in the event of an intruder trying to break into our home. After what just happened, she just became one.

The good thing is the bathroom is in our bedroom suite to the garage. So, the shouting and thumping didn't wake the family room full of kids, resting peacefully on the floor. After putting the gun in the basement recording studio, behind the right 808 speaker on the wall, I returned upstairs to make breakfast. Curious about what Jr. was thinking after witnessing his mother attempting to kill his dad, I wondered how he felt. I've been exhausted because this has been her second or third time trying to kill me. I was trapped with a karmic that death do us part. The day went on without me asking him, as he played basketball with friends and Isaiah out back on the court.

Cleaning the kitchen after making waffles, turkey bacon with egg and cheese, I couldn't help but think of a scene in the movie "Goodfellas" when Henry woke up out of his sleep with Karen sitting on top of him, pointing a gun in his face and accusing him of cheating. Overwhelmed with trying to keep my family together for the children's sake, I'm considering moving out to Atlanta and splitting up with their mother.

Kala and I are having communication and trust issues. Our business is collapsing due to the dysfunction of our relationship. Properties are being forced for sale due to the pre-foreclosure action of the bank. I'm exhausted with managing properties and repairs, dealing with L&I, and the tenants' issues of rent payments. Plus, picking the boys up from school, taking them to practice or workouts in Philly, washing clothes, food shopping, and helping with homework before picking Kala up from work. I felt trapped and alone, isolated from the world with no one to talk to.

My hustle was on hold day after day as I sacrificed my time for the advancement of the family. I would be extremely tired at night, trying to keep my eyes open while driving out of town to pick my money up and drop off drugs like crack cocaine, dope, and weed. Workers wouldn't answer my phone calls when it was time to pay me for the consignment. I felt disrespect all around me, which caused me to shut down personally and close off from the world. Now, mom's mental health has caused her to become more dependent on me.

I don't know what to expect once she is released from the hospital. What will be her physical and mental shape? Can she cook, clean, and use the stairs? I decided to move into mom's house, making repairs and improvements by giving it a fresh coat of paint throughout. I figured this was the least I could do as a son, and I knew she would be surprised and happy to be back at home in a relaxed environment after being released from the hospital. During this time, I could clear my head and focus on the big picture in life—me! I've lost sight of myself and it's time to put me first and prioritize my happiness.

After twenty-three years with someone, you lose sight of replacing "me" with "we" or just providing everyone else's needs and ignoring mine. Don't get me wrong, there's no better job in this world than being a son and a dad. It was something I often wondered if I would be good at because my father didn't want the job or me.

I tried like hell to not allow it to affect my confidence as a child, but it did, especially in sports, not having him to cheer for me in life. My self-esteem as a man without having him there to imitate was compromised. However, the development of my two boys, who are book smart and star athletes, is without compromise.

# FOUR

At the laundromat washing clothes, I emptied my pocket and turned my jeans inside out. I noticed a piece of paper with a number on it—the lady from the hospital. "Oh man," I thought, "I forgot to call... or did I?" Fed up with drama, having someone to talk to and inform me of what to expect could be helpful. If I didn't, she might start mistreating Mom, and I wouldn't even know what she looked like. I had about an hour as the clothes washed and dried.

So, what the heck. 267—I began to dial. "Hello?"

"Yes? I was told to call this number by your co-worker."

"Oh, hi. Is this Ms. Mobley's son?"

"Yes, Seneca. And I'm speaking to whom?"

"I'm Naomi, the tall one. Your mom said I was her favorite."

"Okay, love. How can I help you?"

"I don't need help," she said, laughing. "I think you're cute, and there's nothing more attractive than a man taking care of his mother. My mother had mental issues as well, so I know what you are going through."

"Thanks for that. My mother is all I know. I love her."

"See, that's what I'm saying. Guys nowadays are only worried about themselves or their baby mama drama. You come and see your mom, bringing food and spending time, even when covered in paint and hard white stuff on your arms," she said, laughing.

"That's called compound. It's used when installing sheetrock."

"Oh, you're a contractor?"

"No, I'm a real estate investor who knows a thing or two about carpentry."

"So, you fix your own houses?"

"Yes, that's how you cut costs. I'm looking to buy property and housing for some of these patients. A lot of them don't have family or a place to go once their thirty-day treatment is done."

"Wow, I never thought of that."

"Yes, there's a large demand for housing, and the city pays their rent."

"Okay, let's make a deal. You help me with my mom, and I'll help you find deals in real estate."

"Yes, I was told to go to sheriff sales to get deals."

"Yeah, that's cool if you have money for property repairs. Banks don't like to loan on those types of properties because owners have a right to pay back taxes and reclaim the property within a year."

"See, I knew I was right about you. Thanks. I'll call you later," I said as the bell sounded on the dryers.

"Okay, don't forget," she responded.

Within an hour, I received 20 pictures from her, wanting me to see what she looked like outside of work. What type of car did she drive, what designer bag or clothes did she wear, even guns she owned. Shaking my head, I thought to myself, "Is she crazy or what?" I decided to proceed cautiously, uncertain if her intentions were pure. I didn't reply to texts or phone calls. When I did, it would be in an untimely manner, just to gauge her energy. Calls after business hours were red flags, along with random texts. If Naomi got upset, then she had hidden motives and feelings. I had a lot going on in my life and business, so being a "Chatty Patty" was something I had less time for.

I enjoyed my little peace, and women's attention was something I wasn't lacking. But home was a different story. Nothing was good enough for Kala. I guess I was dealing with a narcissist.

## CHAPTER
# FIVE

Keeping busy with work and family, while trying to focus on purchasing properties, helps get things done. Mother will be released in a couple of weeks, and I'm working overtime to have the property ready. Naomi has been incredibly supportive throughout the transition. However, she felt the need to be more aggressive in her approach toward me. She called to explain that I was sleeping with her, and I didn't know who she really was. How guys be in her DMs offering money just to take her out on a date?

I had to admit she had a dope body and was fly, but after twenty-three years, I'm beyond superficial. I apologized, "Love, I've been crazy busy, but to let you know how much I appreciate you helping, let's go out for a drink later this evening."

What time did she say?" I replied, "Just hit me when you're off work." I got a text from her three hours later saying, "I'm about to get off in 15 minutes. I can come to you since I'm already driving."

"Ok, I'm just finishing up over here cleaning paintbrushes. Text me the address."

"1600 Hollywood Ave. It says 20 minutes, see you soon." Blue Jag car music blasting, pulling up on the curve she hopped out, hair done, nails done, with a tight fit on to greet me smiling with a hug. Then she asked if I minded driving. As she walked around the car for me to see that fat butt to the passenger door, I replied, "Not at all." Not certain where to go or what she likes to eat, I began to drive and ask about her day.

"It was cool, but I can't wait to be my own boss."

"It will happen, love," I responded.

After about 5 minutes, I admitted that I didn't know where I was driving to. I explained that I live in Delaware, so I'm not sure of what spots are jumping on which day. She laughed and entered the location in the car GPS for a hookah bar not far away in the downtown area. The name of the place was Vingo Indian Cuisine and Hookah Bar. We ordered appetizers and drinks.

However, the city was dead due to the SEPTA local transportation strike, so we had the spot nearly to ourselves.

We talked about our day and joked with one another, enjoying each other's company. The food was great as we shared seasoned shrimp with warm alfa bread and hummus. We agreed to end the night early due to our early schedules tomorrow. Finishing our round of Patron, as I sat my glass down, she began to clutch her keys and reach for her pocketbook.

I insisted on paying as we made our way from the booth. I helped her put her jacket on while walking to the door. She replied, "You're such a gentleman," smiling and laughing. As we arrived at my mother's house, laughing at a story she was telling about a co-worker, I parked the car and before I could open the door, Naomi leaned in to kiss me on the cheek. Surprised by it, I blushed and told her, "Call me when you get home, so I know you are safe."

"Okay, handsome."

Man, did the spider sense go off. "Coach, we got one," I thought to myself. How does this keep happening to me? No matter what I do to not engage with women, I'm often targeted by them—often a victim of the thin line between love and hate.

The next day, at 12 noon, I received a call from Naomi.

"I'm just calling to say hi and thank you for being a gentleman last night. Men nowadays just be trying to 'fuck' and offer me money to eat the pussy!!!"

"Wow," I laughed. "You're welcome, beautiful."

"I'm on my way to work. Can I stop by and see you first?"

"If you don't mind seeing me covered in white dust," I explained that I've been sanding walls all morning. "So, I look like a ghost," I laughed.

"A little dust never hurt anybody," she responded. "You're in the direction I take on my way to work, I just want to give you a hug!"

When she arrived, I was in the process of rolling up some weed.

"Step inside," I said.

As she walked up to the door, "Hi handsome," she smiled. "Look at you, hard at work."

"Yeah, something like that," I laughed. "Look at my work, love." As she followed me in, I showed her the improvements that were made around the house.

"You did all of this yourself?"

"Yes, but if I need help, I will bring my boys or hire contractors with experience."

"You do it all, I see. That's why you don't have time for me. But I'm about to change that," she smiled. "Give me a hug!"

"Love, I'm dusty and it's going to get on you."

"Come here and hug me and don't be shy."

Blunt lit, in my mouth exhaling smoke; I palmed her ass while lifting it up.

"Like that?" she responded. "I'm going to come by every day for a hug," she laughed.

"Are you sure you just want a hug?"

She locked eyes with me and began to unbutton my pants fly, pulled out my dick, and started kissing around the head. Mind boggled in disbelief, next thing I know, I'm in the vest of view hitting from the back.

With smoke exhaling from my nose, I long-dicked her for about 5 minutes, trying to keep the ashes from falling in her hair as I pulled it before bussing a nut on her back. She said, "I needed that, Daddy. Now I can go to work with the warm thoughts of you" (laughing).

"Make sure you check on my mom, as I'm pulling my pants up."

"I always do."

Naomi chuckled with a sinister grin. I loved my mother-in-law; I believed that as she walked to the car. What the hell just happened as I got myself together?

I wrapped up work early and headed back home to Delaware. My oldest son, Jr., had a basketball game for his school. I had stopped and picked their mother up from work before getting on Interstate 95 South. We had over twenty-three years together, so affection for one another became a job.

"Hi, Stank."

As she got into the car, "How was your day?"

"Good, just busy,"

"I feel you. Yeah, I see you're covered in dust. Get a lot done?"

"Somewhat didn't get a chance to prime the walls."

"But I plan to have it done along with the floors by tomorrow."

"Great," she responded. "I'm sure your mom is going to be happy. What school does Jr. play again?"

"It's a home game, so we can stop and grab Isaiah. Then go to Wawa to get something to eat and Gatorade."

"Cool, here comes my baby," as the rear right passenger door opens. "Ha, dad, ha, mom," Isaiah says while placing his book bag on the floor behind me.

"How was school?" I asked, looking into the rear-view mirror.

"It was cool, we had a pep rally and I had fun. I'm hungry now, though."

"We are stopping at Wawa before the game," Kala responded.

"Final score 68-72, tough loss, Jr. You played a heck of a game!!!"

"Thanks, Dad. But I don't like this team. The coach plays the upper-class kids as opposed to playing the most talented. He says to wait for my turn for junior and senior year to start. I'd rather move to my grandma's house and attend a school in Philly. What do you think, Dad? Because this team wouldn't make a park pickup game in Philly, chosen league (laughing)"

"Isaiah, what do you think? Y'all trash," (laughing).

"Your mother and I will discuss it. Yeah, Sen, I must talk to my mom first; I'm sure she wouldn't mind the company."

"Home sweet home," as we pulled up and parked in the driveway. As the boys exited the vehicle, walking through the garage, Kala yelled to them, "Wash up for dinner, and do you have homework or assignments needing signing?"

"No, okay, it's late so let's make it quick." Kissing and hugging Isaiah before he got underneath the covers in his vintage Sixers shorts and a short-sleeved t-shirt.

After reading him his favorite Harry Potter book, he asks if I turned the light on in his fish tank.

"Goodnight, Isaiah."

"Goodnight, Dad."

"Dad, did you feed the shark tonight?"

"I'll feed the fish and Mr. Crab before I go to bed. Love you."

"Love you more!!! Goodnight, Jr."

"Goodnight, Dad, can you turn my light off?"

"Yes, and turn that game off after the last quarter."

"Okay!! See you in the morning."

(text) "…thinking of you and that warm nut all on my back… no response, I take it you are home with your family…text me when you're free. I'm doing a double tonight."

What the… I turned my phone on silent as quickly as I could and had it facing down on the marble top vanity. When I hopped in the shower, I felt nervous as hell, so the alerts wouldn't show or sound, hoping she stopped texting me before Kala noticed. I began to replay the event in my head as the water rinsed off the scent and guilt of Naomi. Wondering what I've gotten myself into this time? How is this going to change the dynamic of our relationship? Sex was never part of my plan between us, speaking for myself, but as I suspected, it was a hidden motive.

"Goodnight," with the heart emoji, she texted when I could check my phone, thinking I was done. She got me by the balls, literally, what can she want?

"Goodnight, Kala… Goodnight, Stink… Night."

# CHAPTER
# SIX

Meeting with doctors to discuss the mother's treatment and progress, the head psychologist read me a medical assessment and observation report while I was in their care. The doctor then asked me if there were any issues they may not be aware of. I gave them facts because mom wouldn't let them know what she was experiencing on a daily basis: constant arguing with evil spirits, making food for dead people, and not bathing. Her attitude was aggressive. From sunup to sundown, mother and I were close. I have taken care of her since I was age seven. My father and I were never introduced in my life!

I was told around age eleven he was killed in a botched robbery. His brother stopped by to explain it to my mom while asking if we would like to attend the funeral. I quickly denied the invite. I didn't give two shits about someone I never met. Family to me was my mom and brother. That's who I am dying for. But so far so good, I can relax and stop beating myself up. The meeting was concluded, and a treatment schedule was decided.

Everything is working out for the better. I never had help from family or friends. My brother Zek would stay in his room a lot, listening to music while nodding his head back and forth, even going to sleep when we were younger. But he was the book-smart one, getting A's and a scholarship from Drexel. He would only come outside if someone was messing with me because I was always in the streets. The older guys would bully us from the basketball courts and the corners we stood on.

Trying to earn a buck by going to the store for the hustler. There was always drama in North Philly, and drugs hit our neighborhood badly, causing violence and privation. Mom became a victim of "crack cocaine" as many other parents did in the late 1970s and early 1980s. Her mental state, which I can remember early in my childhood, was a concern for the family.

One time, my grandmother and my aunts tried to force her to get help. I found out later that she was molested as a child by one of her mother's boyfriends. Grandmom refuses to believe her, which causes Mom to suppress emotion and develop the habit of self-medicating. She had us living in the house with no food, gas, and often no electricity. The way we had to survive as kids was insane. They took Zek, at 12, and me, at the age of 8, to my aunt Spuk's apartment uptown to live.

We would have to catch the bus to school and return during the week. One day waiting at the bus stop to return to our auntie's house, I saw my mother sitting on the steps. The bus stop was at the corner of the block where you could see my house. I looked at Zek and said, "I'm not going back, mom needs us." He said, "We got to go back because they are expecting us to return!" I watched mom get up and go into the house, and that's when I told Zek, "I'm going home."

He began to follow me up the street to the house as we yelled out for Mom. We hug and cry as we embrace! She smells like crack, so I guess we surprise her and blow her high. Mother's mental health never seemed to bother Zek; if it did, he never spoke to me about it. Unless she was giving all our toys and bikes away to our friends, saying, "God told her to." A few times we would return from school with all our Christmas gifts gone! I was too young to understand church, but every Sunday we attended Deliverance Baptist church service.

Mom would usher as a volunteer, helping attendees with seating and passing out gospel literature at the end of service. Zek and I were in children's church, but I kept getting kicked out for misbehaving. I really didn't like church growing up, so I would stay with my mother and play tic-tac-toe by myself. Not understanding the "Holy Ghost" or speaking in "tongues," I would sit anxiously for it to end because we would go to Kentucky Fried Chicken afterward.

That was the highlight of the day for me, so much that I would tell my friends. They became interested in joining us on Sunday for church service. She was very kind to our friends, especially the ones less fortunate. She would give them our old clothes, allow them to stay for dinner, or just listen when they needed someone to talk to. It became embarrassing when Mom started using crack.

Our way of life would change drastically!! No longer keeping us up to our usual standards of life. The late toys, bikes, clothes, sneakers, and video games were over for Zek and me. She no longer cared about her appearance—jewelry, fashion, or hair care. Drugs took over Mom's life, and we would never live the same. She stopped doing hair at the house in the kitchen to renting out the extra bedrooms on the third floor. Tenants were friends from the neighborhood who paid on the first and third of the month.

Our house was busy that time of the month because friends were in and out, getting high all day and night. I didn't mind because as a kid, I would be given money for the candy store. We had a tough life but a strong bond between Zek and me. Maybe as the oldest, he was used to seeing her high and crazy. Being four years older than me and having a different dad, maybe it was his escape from having to deal with it. Zek would spend weekends at his dad's house along with his other siblings.

He would come home with new stuff all the time from his dad—outfits, sneakers, and money to spend on whatever he wanted. It used to kill me as a child how my dad thought I wasn't important enough to care for. I didn't have that luxury in life as my brother did, but I knew someday I would obtain it. Drugs were sold on every corner in my neighborhood by the older guys who lived there 24/7 and 365 days. The neighborhood became Beirut, with no one to watch over me. I was around the older guys all the time.

My size made me a formidable target for drug dealers to hustle for them. I was a big young bull with no guidance and starving, going to the store for a dollar or more if they were shooting craps. Because I was allowed to keep the change guessing for good luck, I began to establish trust with them, and I was quickly promoted to holding the drug stash. They showed off their money, jewelry, and cars with rims at the dismissal of high school or at the club let-out.

Often, they would return to me with money in my hand to give them from the sale of the stash I had made. I felt rich as a kid. I had more money than all my friends who were still going to the store for a buck. I had made a buck off every nick I sold out of a thousand dollars pack.

This caused envy not only from my peers, but the older guys that couldn't get on, got high, or just messed up when it came to getting money. The game fell into my lap because all my friends knew my mom or got high at my house!!

I remember one time as a kid, I had awoken from bed to use the bathroom. I could barely see in front of me from all the crack smoke. People were in the hall and on the staircase getting high as if it was a party. I'm in my pajamas, pushing people out of my way, looking for my mom, telling them to get out of my house, crying.

I eventually found my mom in the kitchen, playing cards and drinking beer, looking high. I told her it was time for bed, and everybody had to leave. I poked my chest out as far as a 6-year-old kid could and cleared the house!!! Zek heard me upset telling them to leave, and he came out of his room as I started to see fiends come down the steps. That night, every fiend there remembered and respected me as I got older.

# CHAPTER
# SEVEN

I ended up catching my first case at nine years old for possession with the intent to sell narcotics. I was sitting on my bike, eating a sandwich I'd just bought at the dice game on the corner. I had a pack of crack rocks in my pocket and money for a hustler who had gone to pick up his car from a mechanic shop.

Meanwhile, cops drove up the block the wrong way, creeping. They stopped at the game, demanded the dice, and told us to clear the corner. Before driving off, the officer looked at me and said, "Come here." In panic, I did what he said, not thinking he would search me. Mom ran out of the house over to the police car as the officer placed handcuffs on me. She was upset, hollering, "Let my boy go, he did nothing wrong."

"Ma'am, he is being arrested for possession of a controlled substance."

"What substance? He doesn't have anything to be arrested for!"

Officer Stevens held up a clear sandwich bag containing large vials of crack cocaine. The courts placed me on supervised probation, and I had to report weekly with my school progress report detailing my attendance and participation.

My lust for cash had started out of survival and necessity, leading me to running blocks with my own bricks. Making thousands a day, paying all the bills at home, which led me to introduce my brother to the "dope game." It was out of necessity; see, when the older guys got high off crack and weed, known as turbos, they would try to stick me and others that were inferior.

I was by myself in the streets, playing a game where age doesn't matter. Some of my friends got killed before turning eighteen due to the motivation for cash, murdered in the streets in North Philly. One of my classmates was found in the park in a black Porsche car, lit on fire, only to be identified by the diamond stud earrings he wore.

Summer was heating up the streets for all the wrong reasons, and doughboys all realized times were changing for the bad. The news sent shock waves through the community, and it was later discovered to be a turf war.

Adjusting to the times, I put my brother on to the game, which allowed him to watch my back out here on the block. I showed him what was what and who was who. He started to improve profit margins, so we began to hire workers and shifted up the block with an 8-hour shift clocking 24/7. We made money hand over fist. He was the business, and I was the streets, taking over the neighborhood with $3.00 caps and black tops.

All the OGs' plugs wanted to supply us because I was young with a mind for business. Always ahead of the competition with the best product, giving more, charging less, and respecting the customer with loose change. I often felt bad when serving people who were friends of my mother, especially if they were her company at our house, because I knew they would share with her, so it was as if I was serving her.

Which we never did, however, Mom was slick. She would creep us out of work and cash all the time, claiming we lived with her. "We don't pay rent and sell drugs out of her house, so she should get paid." I'm like only eleven years old paying all the bills now and you're stealing. Mom was a piece of work; guess that's where I get it from—nothing was ever enough, always wanting more, not knowing more money, more problems.

As I was leaving the meeting, I texted Naomi to see if she was at work.

(text) Yes, I'm here.

(text) Where are you?

(text) I'm out front of the hospital in the parking lot.

(text) I'm about to take a break and come down. Give me a second, or you can come up?

(text) I really can't stand the smell of that floor. It smells like death, and you could feel the despair.

Hey, you (smiling), as she exited the revolving door. "How are you?" I asked.

"Okay!! I just left a meeting with the doctors and am now about to go to Home Depot. You're always working," (smiling) "if I don't go get it, it's not going to come to me," (laughing).

"That's true," she responded. "I went downtown today to submit my operation plan to L&I, and they're under review. Prayerfully I get approved. You can help me once I get my property, with repairs and sheetrock," (smiling).

"Sure, love, 'I got you' like I said. Here, give me a hug. I'm about to go back to work. I can't grab that ass like last time," (laughing), "there are cameras and people out," (smiling).

"Boy, give me a hug. I'll call you when I'm getting off. What time are you leaving the city?"

"A little early today because the boys have a workout."

"Okay, super dad," (smiling). "Call me."

Stopping for morning coffee and gas at the station. My phone rings; it's Naomi.

"Hi love, how's your day going?"

"Great," I responded.

"That's what's up. Guess where I'm at?"

"Where?" I asked in a nonchalant tone.

"I'm downtown just leaving City Hall."

"Okay, what's going on there?"

"I was approved by L&I."

"What? I'm so excited! Where are you?"

"I stayed home last night. Basketball workouts ran late. Meet me later to celebrate?"

"Sounds good. I'm excited for you. Way to level up!!!"

Later that day, I received a text: "Let's meet up for drinks. It's happy hour," (laughing).

"Sure, I'm down. North, we can meet at Playmakers Bar and Grill to celebrate the approval of your operation license."

"Okay, where in the north?"

"It's at 29th and Girard Ave. I'm going to GPS it. See you soon."

"Hi Naomi, congrats," (smiling) and hugging. "Yes, it's been a long time coming. Let's go inside, talk all about it, and what is your next step?"

At the bar, pulling out her hair, "This is what bossing up feels like," (laughing).

"I know you know, long as you been a boss," (laughing). "I tell you more money, more problems," shaking my head.

"Give me the problems," she responded, (laughing). After two shots, I was ready to go. I explained that tonight was my baby's mother's 35th birthday, and we'd been trying to work things out.

"I thought you guys were over and done. What gave you that conclusion?"

"Your mother told me about the relationship, and I have been watching how you move!! If she can't recognize a great man, hell, with her, move on."

"Thanks, we plan to go to Atlantic City and spend the weekend together, just the two of us, no kids." I stood up ready to leave, and Naomi said, "Thanks for coming to meet me and celebrate my accomplishment."

"Sure, love, this is what we agreed to help each other out with. Those drinks were strong," (laughing), she said. "I may be too drunk to drive."

"It's only 6:00 PM. How are you too drunk to drive, love?"

"Shut up," she said, (laughing). "Can you take me to my car?"

Like a gentleman, I drove her, and we talked for a few minutes.

"As I explained again, I have plans tonight. We can do something later in the week."

She was unhappy, acting bizarre after 10 minutes. While waiting for her to exit my car, I saw a buddy of mine I hadn't seen in a year.

"Sup champ?"

"Yo, sup man? Park and holler at me!! I'm on my way to 'Yams' to get a drink, want one?"

"Shit, here I come," as I parked and got out of the car, walking across the street.

Naomi is out of the car, moving slowly, (laughing), saying, "I'm drunk, I haven't drunk in a minute."

"You're a lightweight," I responded, (laughing).

"Bet I'm a heavyweight in the bedroom," she replied, (laughing).

"Sup bro, where have you been?"

"Laying low, sucker ducking."

"I feel you, shit's bad out here. I'm about to go get a drink from the speakeasy. This Yam's joint."

"Yeah, her old head got it for her. Where are you and Shorty coming from?"

"Playmakers, them drinks too small around there," (laughing).

"I fuck with Yam's, $10 bucks and have you torn up from the floor," (laughing). "I can't tell Shorty, lit up," (laughing).

"Man tells her to give me the key; I'll drive that fat ass home," (laughing). "She cool, Dee, she is on her way home." Yam's jumping, I noticed, as we crossed the street.

"Yeah, she has been open for a little while now!!" Entering Yam's, we walked up to the bar and began ordering drinks and rounds for my bro and a few other childhood friends and OG's I hadn't seen in a while (laughing). "How's your mom?" they asked. Yam then asked me, "Did I want to get my girlfriend a drink?"

"Girlfriend?" I said. To my surprise, Naomi followed me inside the speakeasy. "What are you doing here?" I asked her.

"I told you I didn't want to drink and drive," she said.

"So, you followed me to get more drinks?"

"No," she replied firmly, "I told you I have somewhere to be. I'm not staying here long."

"It's cool," she said. "You don't want me around you, my feelings are hurt."

"It's not that," I explained, "I'm about to leave the city."

"Oh, why didn't you say that?"

"I did. You asked me to chill while you get yourself together before driving."

"Thanks. See why I like you? Always thoughtful and looking out. I feel safe around you."

Leaving and running late, I called Kala to check her whereabouts and what time to meet her. She was at the dealership getting the car serviced in Wilmington, DE. "When it's done, call me to find out where to meet. It'll probably be downtown by the Ben Franklin Bridge."

"Sure," she responded as we were walking from Yam's. Naomi asked me, "What do you see in your baby's mother? Why do you feel as if there's not somebody out here better for you?"

"I'm saying if after 23 years I'm not married, the person must not be meant."

"Sometimes I do feel that way. However, I have a lot of time invested."

Seemingly disappointed, Sen asked me to drive her to her car. Pulling up next to her car, she began to make accusations about how I was not cool for not getting her home safely. I stated again that I had plans for this evening and wanted to celebrate with her on her accomplishment.

"So, I linked up with you," I added. Then I turned and asked her, "What do you want me to do?"

She asked me to take her on a short ride to get some air, claiming to barely keep her eyes open. I drove to the Art Museum, around the Ben Franklin Parkway, and in about 5 to 10 minutes, I began to feel lightheaded and unable to focus. This was alarming because I hadn't drunk much!

"I'm feeling drowsy, and my vision is off. I see multiple of the same car, driving toward me." Starting to feel paranoid, I turned to Naomi. She was on the phone talking to her girlfriend. I couldn't make out their conversation, but I heard her say, "Girl, I left my gun in the car."

"I'm calling to let someone know who I'm with and what type of vehicle I'm in," she continued. I began to think she was trying to set me up or kill me!

"I'm not driving her back to her car," I decided. As I turned the volume down, I considered going to the airport and checking into a hotel. "That way she can chill, and when she's ready to leave, she can get picked up. Kala can meet me in the parking lot as she passes the airport. Hell, I kill two birds with one stone."

# EIGHT

Check in at the Aloft hotel. I'm sitting on the bottom of the bed while Naomi goes into the bathroom. I started texting Kala to let her know which hotel parking lot to meet me at because I knew I wouldn't be able to drive feeling drowsy and sleepy. I just leaned back and passed out on the bed.

I was awakened by a voice in my ear. "Who is that knocking at the door?" I'm trying to gain consciousness, opening and closing my eyes. I get up staggering to check the door and it's Kala. I thought nothing of it and opened the door to let her in.

"She yelled, 'Where are your pants?'" As I lean back across the bed, shrugging my shoulders.

"Wait, who is this bitch?" Kala yelled furiously. "Naomi, Un, Un... who the fuck is this, Sen? And how the hell does she know what room we are in? Dumb bitch, I went to the receptionist, gave his name, and said I'm his wife."

"Wife!!! Sen, you are married. Get up, get the fuck up," Naomi repeated. I utter no, as things are heating up and beginning to escalate.

"Kala, Sen, what is wrong with you? Get up!" I'm trying to talk and explain but I'm mumbling. I'm thinking, what happened to my pants? I know I didn't get undressed. They began to argue, calling each other bitches and yelling.

I'm trying to get myself together but can't, just too out of it. I can hear the distance between them, but Naomi doesn't know that Kala has hands. I try to get up again, but I keep falling back down. "Get up again," Naomi says, "but I keep falling back down." She says, "Get up and take me to my car!"

"Kala, can't you see he can't drive? How about I call you an Uber?" Naomi replied. "Uber, no, he brought me here, he is going to drive me back," Kala says.

"Sen, this 'bitch is stupid,'" Kala said. "I'm going downstairs to the bar. When I get back, she better be gone or else," Naomi says.

"Fuck you, ugly bitch. All right, be here when I get back," Naomi yelled at me while dialing on her phone. She called her daughter and explained where she was and what happened. As she ended the call, she said to me, "You got me calling my daughter like I'm some lost little girl."

Not sure how much time passed, my old lady returned to the room. "You are still here, now your ride will be an ambulance." I jumped up to get between them, holding up. "Chill," I said, "She called a ride."

"Kala said then she could wait downstairs at the bar or something, but she is getting the hell out of here." I turned to lay back down on the bed. "Boom bap, boom bap." Naomi is holding her eyes as I turn to get back up. "Bitch, I told you to leave," yelling Kala. Naomi stormed out of the room crying, later to discover my wallet.

I told her I would get her a ride, or even take her myself to her car. "She met the wrong birthday bitch today; I don't care about that height shit or that you are bigger than me. I smack that bitch in the face with my phone," laughing. "Man, I'm going back to bed, I'm rock-stat wasted."

After a few hours had passed, I regained consciousness, thinking I just had a bad dream. I'm looking around the room to figure out where am I. Kala is in bed with me, so I'm thinking we're in Atlantic City.

I turned to nudge her to get some sex; she looked at me like a raging bull. "Like you just going to sit there like you don't know what just happened." I'm thinking about what happened and where are my pants. Why do I have my jacket on in the bed? "Boy, get your ass in the shower to wake up. You really were out of it," as she gazes at me toweling off sitting on the side of the bed.

As I took a deep breath, she looked me in the face, staring into my eyes. "Are you telling me you really don't know what happened tonight?" "What happened?" I responded.

As there's a knock at the door!! "Who is it?" "The police, open the door!!" I turned to look at Kala, like what the fuck across my face. "Police." "What the hell do they want?" shaking my head. She said, "Maybe that girl called them." "What girl," I asked. "That bitch you had here." "Bitch I had here? We're not in Atlantic City?" "No, we're at the airport in the room you booked." "Police open, one second getting dressed." "What happened?" "That bitch wouldn't leave, so I beat her ass up."

"What bitch?" I opened the door, and the detective asked my name and said that this room was a crime scene. I asked why and what happened.

"Detective, that's what we're here to figure out. Your name and miss?" "What's the crime officer," I asked repeatedly. "Can you talk to me, this is crazy." As detectives surrounded us, they instructed us to put on our shoes and come with them.

They led us to the elevator through the lobby outside, placing us inside of a park police jeep. The officer radioed another police cruiser parked across from us.

I saw the headlights flash twice and the detectives pulled us out of the vehicle and placed us both under arrest for rape and assault. The wind knocked out of me, in disbelief of the ordeal.

"I'm Detective Grey, and you both have the right to remain silent, and anything you say can be held against you." My head is spinning, what the hell is going on? "Rape and assault?" "Who the fuck did I rape? This shit doesn't make any sense." "Assault who?" Kala whispered, "Chill, this bitch just lied to us." "That bitch lied?"

"That tall bitch you had in the room. I don't remember anything other than waking up to you." We arrived at the Special Victim Unit and they put us in separate cells, one officer said they didn't want us collaborating on our stories.

They interrogated us one by one. Kala first came back and tried to yell down at me. "Bitch said I hit her in the face with my cell phone after she called me ugly," saying I was mad because she wouldn't have a threesome with us. "Yo, are you kidding me, this shit can't be real?" "It's real Sen, so don't lie to them." "Lie? I don't even know the truth."

Cell opened, Mobley the cop shouted!! I exited, walking toward the detective. "Have a seat! I'm Detective Gray and I'm with the SVU Special Victims Unit. Do you know a young lady by the name of Naomi?"

"Yes, she works at the hospital where my mother was staying. She claims you two assaulted her and forced her to engage in a sexual threesome," he explains. "You took her to a hotel claiming to be sick? Once in the room, you and Naomi started having sex."

"It was a knock at the door. You answered, and in return with your wife, she quickly objected, wondering how Kala even knew y'all were there. She tried to get dressed, but you guys jumped her. Kala hit her in the face with her cell phone, knocking her on the bed. You jumped on top of her and pinned her down to the bed. Somehow, she escaped, leaving with your wallet. Do you recall any of this, Mr. Mobley?"

"Vaguely," said the officer. "No, Detective Gray, I'm not certain about much tonight because I believe I was drugged. My old lady had been upset with me all night about me being in a hotel room and having my pants off with a girl. I'm thinking no way I would get caught like that, creeping then calling my old lady and letting her know where, shit doesn't make sense."

"The door opened; the cop entered and handed the results back from the DNA sample. 'Detectives, look like we have a match; potassium from the semen found in her vagina matches your DNA. What do you have to say about that?'"

"I mean all I remember is a soft voice coming from over top of me saying, 'there is someone at the door.' I tried getting myself together before I got up, knock, knock, the voice repeated itself. 'Who knows we are here?' Naomi said. I opened the door, and it was Kala; to my knowledge, nothing was going on so there was nothing to feel guilty about letting her in. She asked me where my pants were."

"The only thing I can think of, Detective Gray, is Naomi had taken off my pants and was riding on top of me as I laid back passed out asleep on the bed. How else would I think a voice came from over the top of me? Okay, how did your wife know where to find you?"

"We were going to Atlantic City for her birthday, so we were meeting there and riding over together. How did she know what room? I don't know. What about the assault? Did you jump on top of her and pin her down forcing yourself inside her as your wife watched?"

"Hell no, I was the one in bed sick as a dog. Is it possible to take a blood test? Take my blood because I feel like I have been drugged. This whole night seems like a nightmare I can't wake up from." Detectives said too much time had passed to check my blood for any prescription-based drugs.

"I can't remember a thing, and I don't want to say anything that can incriminate me. Fine, we are done here; take him back to the cell." Bail was set at $50,000 for Kala and $100,000 for me with a stay-away order and no contact with the plaintiff, the judge explained.

"I'm thinking of my boys at home with my mother, who is mentally disabled to take care of them because both of the parents are booked with their bail set at $150,000. I'm in the county jail still dazed and confused. Why would Naomi do this to me, set me up like this? She knows my mother only depends on me."

"I'm stressing in this orange jumpsuit while eating the foul food. The juice was so bad it would stain the floor if spilled, so imagine what it did to my stomach. I would lay on the bottom bunk and think to myself how I got here. Not in jail but in my decision-making, slipping and getting caught up like this. But I should have known better than to make plans with Kala because the last time we tried to reconcile it ended badly."

"Returning home from a dinner date with the pair, she began to assault me as she parked. Shouting, snapping, and insinuating that I didn't love her and didn't want to be here anymore. In rage, hitting me in the face, I got out of the Benz and ran to my work van to avoid the argument in front of the neighbors. She drove up the driveway, hitting me and ramming the bumper of the van. I pulled off cutting across the lawn at high speed as she followed. The mine van wasn't a match for the Mercedes Benz she drove as she pulled in front to cut me off."

I stopped before she could make a U-turn in a driveway going the opposite direction. I drove around a sharp curve on the road and parked, turning off the headlights. The next thing I knew, she came around the curve at high speed, losing control and causing the vehicle to flip over in the air and land over train tracks into a barn. I jumped out in panic for her life and ran over to the R 350, flipped upside down with her alive in one piece. We went home, and I nursed her scars as we thought of a story to tell the police.

Kala had alcohol in her system from dinner and could not get a DUI because of her job. I often thought while in here if she would leave me to riot because it involved a girl again. But Kala didn't understand how frustrating it was to give my all to someone who wouldn't forgive past transgressions. She began cheating at work with co-workers, returning home with her underwear in her bag. Texts between unknown numbers said she dreamed about them all while sleeping next to me. As it's said, "Once A Good Girl Gone... She's Gone Forever," I had to live with the fact I did her wrong forever.

Praying for an answer from God, and after about two weeks, my bond was posted. The old lady got out first because her mother and sister put up their house and cash with the bail bondsman. Once she was home, she put up our house and got the rest of my cash off the street. My cousin Bam helped with the rest because I was still short a couple of hundred. All the while, I'm thinking to myself, I've got to leave this toxic situation at home. I could be in jail for murder and wouldn't have a clue what the hell happened.

Home, excited to be with the boys and see my mother. "Thank God," nothing tragic happened to them while being detained. But when I went back to the hotel to get my rental car, it was destroyed. Windows busted all around the truck. Naomi keyed it and took all my valuables with the clothes I brought to wear in AC. This nightmare of a situation won't end. The additional cost for repair and pants was $3,500.00. Nothing was off-limits to Naomi. I wanted to know what and how this happened.

I can't call her because of the no-contact clause in the bill. I could go back to jail, forfeit my bond, and lose my home. A few days have passed, and I can't get any rest until I speak to Naomi. I have thought about showing up at her job, but cameras catching her in traffic as if I were passing and stopping her. I'm wrecking my head, not eating, and stressing. This shit has ruined my home and any thoughts of getting back with Kala, especially when she was in county jail. They made her put on a vest with straps that tied down her hands and arms. The C.O. said it was due to the charges. They considered her a high-level custody danger. She said she was cool though; all the female prisoners feared her because of the way staff treated her. Little did they know that this was the first time she'd been to jail. We laugh, but I think it's mainly her mother and sister; they never liked me anyway.

They knew I had a street reputation because of the letters from the juvenile jail Kala would receive. "Why can't you date someone with a common background and not this hoodlum?" She was often asked by her mother if she felt that Kala could do better, with her being provided for school and from a good family. Her sister started to dislike me because I got Kala to set up her neighbor from across the street. He was a big mouth who believed he could say what he wanted about me because he got on by stealing cars and he liked her.

Getting money from it, I told Kala to act as if the feeling were mutual and sit outside with him. I would have my shooter come up to rob him, and you just play it off. Word eventually got out after people from their neighborhood saw me driving his car. Her older sister Nattily was very concerned for Kala's welfare once she heard the rumors and believed she was in danger of retaliation. She believes I was a bad influence and a thug. Needless to say, I would have off whoever caused Kala harm. I stood in the middle of their neighborhood barber shop with a tech 9 machine gun clip hanging outside, expressing it. If one hair is touched on her, it's on. I met Kala when we were fifteen on Memorial Day at the cookout, and we have been together for over twenty-five years, although we were never married. I considered Kala my wife. Her family never changed their mind about me, even though it's been two grand-boys, economic achievement, and relocating to our new home in Delaware that is over 5,000 square feet. I would never be good enough to gain their acceptance or approval in their family.

Friday afternoon, I received a phone call from a restricted number. When I answered, I thought it was my P.O. telling me to come in. I'm on probation for a few pounds of weed! Me having police contact and being charged with rape and assault would violate my probation. "Hello," I answered. "It was silent." Hello? Hello? I just hung up. The phone rang again. "Hello?" This time a female answered and said, "You don't know me, but we have a mutual friend, and she wants to talk to you." "Sure," I responded. As I heard the phone being passed, "Hello, yes, it's me, Naomi." My first reaction was to hang up, but I needed clarification on what had happened that night. I responded remorsefully, "Hey, love, you okay? What happened that night between us?" She explained her actions were based on my old lady showing up, being disrespectful, and hitting me in the face with a phone. I was embarrassed to call anyone to take me back to my car with my face bruised. So, I told my daughter when she arrived I was raped, take me to the SVU.

It used to be located at the hospital where I worked, so I knew exactly what to tell them. "What about my mom?" The fact that she just came home, and you knew how much she depended on me. You should have thought of that before you called Kala. You let wifey know where you were and did not protect me. "That bitch hit me in the face with a phone, so I hit those pockets," (laughing). "That time you FaceTimed me with your mother, I noticed your house and how nice it was. I figured that would get back at her. To be honest, it wasn't even for you, but I had to tie you into the story because I didn't have an address on her. I had her Philly address but that's her mom's house." So, I took your wallet as I ran out of the room. "I apologize, love, for this whole situation."

I had no idea what took place. I actually felt drugged that night because I don't remember any of this. "In fact, why were we at the hotel? She said I wanted to spend time with you, so I drugged you. I kept acting like I was too drunk to drive, but I was waiting for the drugs to kick in. Knowing you wouldn't leave me; don't worry I am going to court about this nut shit. The charges will be dropped as long as you act right? Act, right? I repeat it." "Yeah, you bet not have sex with her until this case is over. I still like you and I want to finish what we started before she showed up."

"Yeah, that was crazy, I had no pants on when she came into the room. I know when I got out of the shower, you were passed out on the bed. I took your pants off, started sucking your dick, and sat on it riding you. Just when it was starting to feel good, and I was ready to come, I hear a knock on the door, which explains the voice coming from over the top of me." "Yup, and with you being inside me I had to come from you that supported my story."

"Well, thank you for letting me know what happened. Because detectives charged me with 'Rape and Assault.' I knew this couldn't be me, I'm too fly of a person to be taking pussy." "She giggled and said, 'don't let this stress you, I just wanted to get her back somehow.' My feelings were hurt, and I was embarrassed when my daughter saw my face. I understand thanks for calling me because I was stuck."

"I didn't know how to get in contact with you after that night. 'What do you mean all you had to do was buy a burner phone?' Like I did to call you, thanks!! I guess that shit is crazy. I must go, love, my son has a game, so I'll talk to you later." "Okay, I'm around just call me because I can't call you. I'm going to call you back and unblock the number. Just call this phone!"

"Hitting my pockets, Naomi. After bail, we were broke and I considered having a public defender to represent me and a court-appointed lawyer for Kala at the preliminary. Later that night, after the game, I told Kala I received an anonymous call today while she was at work." "This bitch is crazy, I'm going to show you how to play this bitch. I'm thinking in the back of my mind, haven't you done enough? Stuck between a rock and a hard place? I'm not certain what to do to get from underneath this. Moreover, I must see my probation officer next week."

"On Tuesday morning, I have an 11 am appointment with P.O. Roberts, a young guy with whom I had a good reputation. When I arrived at the receptionist, I told her who I was there to see. She instructed me to sign in and take a seat. I was nervous because you just never know when or if you're going to get locked up every time vesting." "I sat in the waiting area for my name to be called, looking at my phone every minute. I sent a text to my oldest son detailing my personal bank account information, passwords, and secret hiding places to look just in case I am arrested."

"'Mr. Mobley?' I responded, 'Yes?' I got up to walk to room #5. Roberts was sitting at the desk typing on the computer. 'Have a seat, Mr. Mobley.' 'Thanks, Mr. Roberts.'" "Sure," as he turns back to the screen to look over my file. He asked if there's been any change in my employment or residency. "No, everything is the same. Great, has there been any police contact?" "I first started to lie; however, I wasn't certain if he knew already. I was damn if I do and damn if I don't tell him about the situation."

Taking a deep breath and exhaling, I began to explain to him the altercation and circumstances of the charges. He felt compassion for me and the situation, but through protocol, he had to discuss it with his supervisor. Excusing himself, he exited the room and secured the door. I started to feel claustrophobic as I sat in the chair in this small room. The door locked behind you once you entered and could only be opened by P.O. with the push of a button located on a string around his neck. The thought of walking out and leaving was a no-go.

About 15 minutes had passed, and I was certain he would return with officers to handcuff me and place me in the holding cell. However, he returns with a slight grin on his face, still in disbelief at my story.

"I talked to my supervisor, and I want to first thank you for being straight up with me. These charges hadn't shown up yet in our computer system, but had they been, and you didn't tell me, I would have recommended your arrest."

"Instead, you are free to keep me informed on the situation."

"I'm free to go?" I asked.

"Yes, had the charges been drugs or possession of a firearm, you would have been a repeated offender who would have violated probation."

"See, I was placed on probation because of possession with intent to deliver a controlled substance — marijuana."

"Thanks," as I gave him a head nod, standing up to leave.

# TEN

Preliminary hearing at court today, and I'm nervous about the outcome. It's our third time at court, and Naomi kept her word to not show up. This means that the case could be dismissed for no show of the plaintiff.

As we're parking in the lot, my phone rings.

"Hello? It's me, is she next to you?"

"No, why? What's up?"

"Sorry, but today I'm showing up for court. Or they will put a warrant out for my arrest and revoke my license to carry a firearm."

"What does that mean? My life is on the line and you're willing to lie to me? Did you say the entire time things were a lie? What changed?"

"Well, you really don't call me anyway, so I guess y'all trying to work things out and be a family. I told you not to do that, I want you to be with me and you on her side now. I told you; I told you. Leave that bitch alone and start loving me like you love her."

In disbelief, I think to screenshot the text and forward it to my attorney. Hoping this will prove that she is conversing with me and still wants to see me, if we are ordered to stay away from each other, this should prove she is violating the judge's orders.

My attorney replied and said there was nothing he could do about it because it would show that both of us violated the order. To my surprise, he told me to keep talking to her, hoping she would slip up and change her story. This is some insane crazy psychotic scene out of the movies, I'm thinking.

When entering the courtroom, I couldn't look at Naomi because I was furious that she showed up, just to tell lies about me and drag this case out. If I had known she would not keep her word, I would have stolen, robbed, and borrowed to hire a private attorney. Never had I used a public defender to represent me in court.

As we are instructed to rise for the Honorable Judge Mitchell, grounds for a trial were granted and we are to report back to court next month. We left the courtroom and waited in the hall for the elevator. Naomi and her teenage daughter walked by us to the rest area. I grab the old lady's hand showing unity, I don't give a fuck about what she thinks or trying to do to me. Nobody is controlling me, not her or this attorney.

With all this trouble surrounding me, I can't help but reflect on a spiritual reading I received from a "Haitian spiritual reader." She warned me of involvement in relationships that were having a negative impact on my life and business. That's why my dearest relationships involve me being dependent on and used with no reciprocation. She compares it to leeches sucking me dry.

My mother lived her life, and I need to live mine. Do not, I repeat, do not get involved with her mental health issues. Because you will pay a heavy price and damage will be catastrophic to your immediate family. My brother will have to fend for himself in this world. It's not your responsibility to stop him from dealing drugs and hustling in the streets. Don't incorporate him in your future real estate endeavors.

Whatever we did to survive back then, was back then leave it in the past. She also told me to move out of my home because my spouse is not for me. I said we just brought that house off of "DJ Jazzy Fresh" for a million dollars. She insisted I leave, or I would pay a heavy price if I didn't follow her instructions. Explaining it was a curse placed, on me and she gave me two options. One was returned to sender to who sent it to me or just removed from it, releasing it back into the world.

I was then instructed to remove my shoes and clothes down to my underwear. Her assistant picked up out of a clay vessel with her hands. They began to wipe my body from my neck to my feet with fire to burn the leeches off as she spoke in "Haitian tongues." The revelation was mind-blowing, it caused me to evaluate my involvement in my dearest relationships. Boy, was she right about these life events?

Later I found out in his own emission that Zek, stole from me for years. I would trust him unconditionally. Often felt he was stashing on me but could never prove it, I eventually did and swore to never do business with him again. It taught me a big lesson, that money will cause greed and family doesn't mix with business. One time I got so upset that I pulled an AK-47 out on him demanding he give me my money. Mom jumped in between us screaming and pledging for me to put the gun down. Eventually, I did and vole to kill him if he tried me again.

Seeing through the whole ordeal, Kala has been helping me see things from a female perspective. And why Naomi would do some foul shit like this. I must admit, it was great focusing on an issue other than being at odds with one another. However, when Kala pointed out issues and characteristics about Naomi, I could not help but think about what she had been doing to me this whole time. Women are scandalous, and social media is the field of play.

After getting the bailout, to my surprise, Kala started posting pictures with captions that would reflect as if she was no longer in a relationship with me. This was brought to my attention by friends and family that followed her. They called to question me and asked if everything was good between us, to my knowledge it was. At least I thought from a public view, thinking to never speak about home life to the public.

But this one phone call I got from my girl cousin suggested that I was "fooling myself." She said go to social media and check out her page. I did as we talked on the phone, and I was in for a rude awakening!! Half-naked pictures with inviting captions!! (It's still my birthday, who's trying to cash out?) I agreed the caption was inappropriate for someone in a relationship. Cousin, I'm starting to worry about you, and if you need me, I'm here for you. Thanks, cousin, let me go; I need to get to the bottom of this.

When I brought it to Kala's attention later that day at home, she downplayed it, claiming that if I had a page, I would understand social media. But because I'm a drug dealer and I don't do phones, I'm being insecure. You're right, knowing what doesn't come out in the wash will come out in the rinse. Her mother and father had a toxic relationship, one which involved adultery and financial issues due to her reckless spending on jewelry and summer homes.

Issues that started to resemble our lifestyle were the constant arguing in front of the kids, cops being called to the house, and cheating on one another. Kala's lack of support and involvement disrupted our real estate investment company. The majority of the properties were in her name; I was still hustling drugs in different towns. So, if something happened to me for the worst, my family would be in good shape to maintain the life they were accustomed to. Therefore, I'm thinking I should leave this relationship. It's not like they are babies; they are old enough to call me and communicate their needs and wants.

Saturday basketball game for our youngest son Isaiah, we arrive at the gym late due to Kala and I arguing this morning. Upset I came in late without calling her; the drive over we barely said two words to each other. Which was not alarming because she would be texting or strolling on social media. What she didn't know was that I'd seen messages of her texting other parents on the team. Not sure who it was until I did a little research and dialed the number from the messages off my phone.

As I push the dial, the name out of my contact pops up! Not my man; his son and my son are friends plus I speak to his wife whenever I see them at the gym. Can't wait until I run into him and give him a piece of my mind. Not about the tiptoeing around but you not going to be shaking my hand, rubbing my son on the head, and smacking my assume "bitch" on the ass. While waiting for the game to start, Kala's co-worker was at the gym watching his son just finished playing. The way she smiled and greeted him annoyed me because I hadn't recognized him or been introduced.

I watched them talk until halftime as I stood under the basket to motivate Isaiah. She never liked to sit by me because she would say that I was too loud and embarrassing when yelling at the referees for a bad call. Walking down the other end of the court I passed them and asked her if she was there to see her son play. She replied yes and tried to introduce me to her co-worker Jodi. I wasn't interested in meeting him; I turned and walked away. I'm not shaking any man's hands that you could be smashing on the low. When the game was over, I was heated; they stood together the whole game talking. I'm not sure if it was jealousy, embarrassment, or the cocktail drink I had.

As we drove to Philly, the arguing began again; calling each other out of our names and shouting in front of Isaiah was not a good look. I was tired of being the bigger parent; I first thought sitting in the back seat by Isaiah would keep me cool. I guess the feelings I was trying to suppress came to a head. Kala secretly was videoing me arguing and upset with her in an aggressive behavior. As we neared her mother's house, she pulled into the police station hoping to get me arrested by showing them the video of us arguing. I jumped out of the jeep behind her and followed her inside the district.

The officer Kala stopped I knew from our oldest son playing AAU basketball. He pulled me to the side and explained that it was best to walk away, clear my head, calm down, and talk to her later about the issues that were causing me to feel disrespected and upset. Thanks for the advice as we shook hands; I then began to walk to the park.

# ELEVEN

Trial begins today, and Naomi takes the stand, trying her best not to look at me. I turned my head away when she started her statement. I knew it was all lies, but I was still embarrassed and ashamed. The deputy officer of the court was once my neighbor in my early childhood years. She couldn't believe I was caught up in a situation like this. The judge is my back judge from a drug case in which I was found guilty of possession with the intent to distribute that happened over fifteen years ago.

I'm trying not to look at anybody in the face as I sat inhumation. As she speaks, Naomi begins the story of the altercation between her and Kala. She is then cross-examined by Kala's attorney. He finds her story contradictory to the statement she gave in the police report. The more she talked, I noticed she was trying to keep me out of it. We had not talked since the preliminary because I could no longer allow to be manipulated by her. The court was in recess and scheduled for a later date.

Feeling the tension at home, I moved back to Philly. I'm staying with my mother until the case blows over. Mom was happy to have me there even though I would stop by every day and check on her. A habit I got from my 8th-grade teacher Mr. Thomas El. He always stopped and checked on his mother when dropping us off from basketball practice.

The phone rings while I'm unpacking my belongings in the rear bedroom. "Hello?"

"Hello, this is Naomi."

"Yeah, I answered what's up?"

"I wanted to apologize for court the other day."

"What do you mean? This isn't the first time you've shown up. You don't keep your promises, we both know that."

"Let me make it up to you."

"How?"

"I want to take you to dinner."

"Man, I can't trust you."

"I'm sorry, I felt like shit lying on the stand."

"Where do you want to meet?"

"You picked the place since you don't trust me."

"Listen I'm just not for the B.S. You can pick the spot; I trust you enough for that."

"Ok, I'm going to check and see what's open because it's kind of late."

"Bet, call me back!"

When I hung up the phone, I thought to myself she probably set me up for some payback. Nothing like a damaged woman whose strap gives her a license to carry.

We met at a place we both felt comfortable at, a place with cameras that could record our behavior. The restaurant was in the northeast section of Philly, in a predominantly white neighborhood. When I arrived, I pulled up in the parking lot under the cameras, feeling I had to do something to prove my innocence. Then it hit me: agree with her and sympathize with her feelings.

I walked up to her as she got out of her car. I looked to see if she was packing her gun; her outfit would have revealed it if she was, wearing a one-piece bodysuit with hills and carrying a clutch purse. Entering the restaurant, I noticed it was inside a hotel. I held the door as we entered, greeted by the hostess. We got seated at a booth so that we could talk in private. I sat with my back to the kitchen facing the door by the window to see the cars come and go out of the parking lot. You could never be too careful, especially after what Kala opened my eyes up to.

I begin by saying, "That you're right to be upset; you are the victim in this situation because I didn't protect you. I'm deeply sorry for that," looking into her eyes. "But let me know why you wanted to meet me tonight."

Shit, I forgot now after you just hit me with that apology. No, but...the waiter interrupts, asking for our order. We ordered drinks first as we talked to feel each other out. She had Cîroc vodka and cranberry and I had Red Bull and Remy Martin neat. You guys ready to order the waiter asked, the kitchen was about to close. Yes, we would like to start with the crab dip and nachos. She will have a Caesar salad with chicken. Look at you ordering my food for me. See you thought I didn't remember, (laughing). I'll take this shrimp and grits with cheese and red onion if you have it. I'll check Sir, will that be all, the waiter asked? We looked at each other and decided on another round of drinks (laughing).

As I was saying, I wish that night didn't end like that. I wanted you inside me all night. Yes, because I would have had you looking for me in the daytime with the flashlight (laughing). Boy, whatever, you know you wanted it. With your busy ass self, always working or with your boys. I noticed you said wanted, like past tense. What do you mean? I mean like how do you know I don't still want it, (laughing). Is it too late? As the waiter brought out our food and placed it on the table. Never she responded.

She says I have something for you as she gets up to go to the trunk of her car and returns with a white bag. It was my new outfit I was going to wear in Atlantic City for Kala, birthday. Thanks, I said smiling, I saw she was pressed and after a few more drinks, I got up to sit next to her. I put my hand on her inner thigh and gave her a compliment in her ear "You look like the Goddess Ice's."

She kissed my cheek and began to tell me "She'd been wanting me in the worst way." So, I told her to get us a room. Why, she said? Are you going to stay the whole night with me? Sure, and you can have me the way you want me.

She got excited. But I said it's one thing. What? "I don't have any credit cards, I'm using cash." We'll pay for dinner, and I'll get the room on my credit card. Bet, see I was plotting. I knew that later I would tell my attorney she paid for the room at the hotel for us to have sex. Man, I beat the brakes off that pussy for hours. I put her in positions she hadn't been in since a teenager. She went right to sleep, and I slid off. Not before I took pictures of her sleep, condoms used on the bed, and the room number of the hotel.

The next morning, I called my attorney to update him about the event. Told him in full detail what happened between us and pictures to prove it. Phone beeps and Naomi calls asking me where about. See I knew you weren't going to wake up to me. Where are you? Apologies love, I had an important meeting this morning. On a Sunday, she asked? Yes, I had to meet with the roofers for an estimate. Okay, I'm going to get up soon before checkout let's get breakfast. Sounds good, hit you when I'm finishing up over here. Hell, what that, knowing I'm done with her.

String her along in the weeks to come, sending her flowers at work and endless sexual phone conversations leading up to court. I needed to keep a pulse on her to make sure she didn't think our time spent wasn't genuine.

CHAPTER

# TWELVE

Court today, and Kala and I haven't spoken for weeks. I considered calling her often about what happened, but that could have made matters worse between us. I sat a few rows behind Kala in the courtroom, smiling every chance I could at Naomi. The case was called, and we were instructed to stand for the judge. My attorney asked all parties to approach the bench. Kala looked at me with concern. I hadn't told her about the date with Naomi—how would I explain it?

I sat there, cool, calm, and collected. I knew I had this case over and done. He began to show the judge and DA his phone with the pictures I sent to him. They looked at me, then at Naomi, and turned back around, whispering to each other. As the DA returned to his seat, he leaned over to inform Naomi about the new discovery. She looked over at me with a look of betrayal as she shook her head. I smiled and asked my attorney, "What now?" He explained the judge was reviewing the new evidence and deciding on a verdict.

I felt anxious as he and Kala's attorney shared notes back and forth on what grounds the DA had to pursue the case. Kala was updated on the situation and remained calm, putting her hands together. I wasn't certain what she was thinking or if she was mad at me about the news. I could only hope she understood my actions and that I'd done it for us.

Court was back in session, and the judge went on to say, "So now the question became if your client felt threatened, raped, and assaulted by the defendants, then why go for a night on the town with him and pay for it?" Naomi couldn't explain her actions or behavior to the DA or the judge. Her daughter jumped up in disbelief, "My mother was raped, and y'all not going to do anything about it." "Order in the court," the judge said, banging the gavel. "One more outburst from you, young lady, and I will find you in contempt of court." "Fuck your contempt, that's my mother," as tears ran down her face.

Naomi stood up to hug her. As she sobbed, "It's not fair, Mom," she explained to her daughter that she had wrongfully accused us of the charges. She pulled back from Naomi with a look of confusion on her face. "Mom, you are telling me that you made the whole thing up. How could you? Why destroy these people's lives?" Looking defeated and exhausted before she could reply, the case was dismissed without prejudice, and I never spoke to Naomi again.

Things at home were irreconcilable; trust was out the door forever. Later that day at the house, while I'm packing the rest of my clothing in boxes, Kala asked me about the night that episode took place between Naomi and me. I responded that the when doesn't matter, only the why. I had to take the law into my own hands; fuck a public defender. We were facing life if convicted on these charges. What if our boys would've grown up parentless as we rotted in a cell? No fucking way will my kids see me in jail at a visit behind glass on a phone.

I got us into this situation; it was up to me to get us out. As I walked to the door, I stopped to kiss her forehead, hoping my explanations and apologies were enough to ask for forgiveness. I knew she didn't have the strength to leave me after all these years, but I knew it was best that I left and moved on with life, with hopes of becoming the best co-parents in the world.

The End.

"I'm trying to figure out the social media. Out, Jr.? Dad here, let me see. You are all set. Just add a picture to your profile."

"What does this mean, Sen? You have a friend request. You can click on their profile to check pictures before accepting."

"Okay. Poison Ivy. Who is this? Oh, this bitch had the nerve to send me a friend request."

Sincerely

**Seneca Willoughby**

I appreciate the wait, and I'm sure you will enjoy this must-read fictional thriller, 302.